DEFINING MOMENTS

Meenakshi Sundaram Hariharan

ACKNOWLEDGEMENTS

Thanks to my wife Shubhashree for the inspiration behind my writing habit.

Thanks to my son Aditya for being the inspiration to become inquisitive.

Thanks to Vijayashree for introducing me to medium.

Thanks to my friend and mentors Ms. Rama and Mr. Raghu Iyer for providing inputs on what I write.

Thanks to my niece Shruthi for designing the cover page.

INDEX

PENCIL DROPPING MOMENT

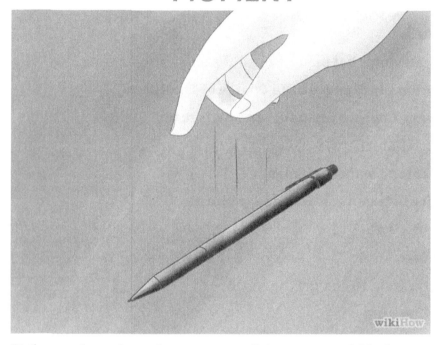

"Why you keep dropping your pencil?". My Mom chided me.

"What is wrong in dropping a pencil?"—I thought to myself.

This habit of dropping pencil while the teacher gets engrossed in the class continued. It was a momentary fun to escape from the world of mathematics or history to a world of solitude. Until one day when a teacher noticed me and called me for a talk.

Blaming myself for not being careful, I entered the teacher's cabin.

"I know you love dropping pencil. But you know what happens during that time. You miss something important in the lesson. The point which you can capture and keep it in your mind forever whiskers away and you toil yourself to get that point grilled into your mind".

Teacher made her point. I realised the mistake only when the marks were out. Pencil dropping stopped. or at least I thought so.

Last week, My wife attended District Annual Toastmasters Conference in Bahrain. I went to pick her after the conference. She was jubilantly describing the events to me, when I noticed my son doing some tricks in the car. My attention got distracted and I told my son to stop doing that.

He got upset. But that was not the only thing that happened. My wife got upset.

"You always do this whenever I talk. If you are not interested in the first place, why pretend listening"

"No, I am still listening to you"

"I cannot speak now as you spoiled the conversation" She shut down the conversation.

Is this a pencil dropping moment. Yes, it is.

How many times we do come across such pencil dropping moments in our daily life. Some of the pencil dropping moments that I have experienced (Actually, I am the culprit in few cases)

People playing with mobile phones while having conversation .

People who check emails while having a discussion.

People who leave the conversation in the middle only to have another chat with someone else.

People answering mobile phones while in a conversation without even bothering to apologize.

When we submit ourselves to our mind wandering in some place else while someone else is intently and intensely engaged in a meaningful conversation with us. Are we adding meaning to the conversation and the relationship or do we allow the pencil dropping moment to rob us the joy of engaging relationship.

I do have this habit of checking mails while attending phone calls. One of my colleague commented "Something interesting happened or is there a new mail that has disturbed you". It hit me straight in my face. I stopped reading mails while answering phone calls from then on.

What are the Pencil Dropping Moments that keeps repeating in your life and what action you want to take to avoid these moments.

SCRATCH

That day started as usual. Great expectations, hopes and aspirations like every other day. I got ready for my morning ritual - walking. Listening to the audio book stored in my mobile with the headphones, I took the shoes.As I wore the shoes I noticed something strange..new shoe (ok..it is 5 months old but for an Indian anything less than 5 years is considered new) suddenly appeared rugged. Few scratches on the shoe making it appear old. I started wondering how this happened. I used it two days back when it rained. The shoe became muddy. I remember having kept in the washing room to clean.Oops..it should be the maid. She has washed the shoes and cleaned it using the brush.

How do you feel when you realise someone has scratched your new shoes? or Having spent considerable money to buy , it was spoiled by an inadvertent or ignorant action of the maid. First emotion that sprang in me was anger. I moved on to complete my ritual - walking. When I returned home, to discover that the anger had evaporated. However, still I made sure the message is sternly passed on to the maid not to carry out such misadventures in future.

This episode left me pondering about how emotions determine our actions and decide the course of our lives. If the scratch has happened because of my action, I would feel guilty. But because the scratch is the outcome of someone's ignorance or inefficiency, evokes anger and the scratch due to a superior force like boss, would leave me with suppressed emotion, fuming inside. In all three emotions will leave me broken.

Anger not only consumes the power inside me but also creates a ripple effect. It engulfs the other person in hurt and accelerate the anger in that person. Anger creates more anger. It becomes a relay race in anger.

Guilt is a pernicious disease. It will steadily and gradually kills the individuals internally by annihilating the self-respect.

On the other hand, helpless feeling leaves one with anger that eats internal peace gradually. It is like a Pressure cooker. The Pressure manifests itself at an unwanted time spewing anger. This leaves the closer ones vulnerable to the unexpected outbursts.

Watch the emotion that springs inside. Are these emotions helpful or hurtful.

I am reminded of a fantastic speech by my friend Aditya Maheswaran, a Champion Speaker and Management Consultant . He spoke about scratch. A glimpse of his speech is produced in the below video.

The scratches are inevitable and we end up creating scratches. But like Aditya mentioned the scratches will only remain until we polish it. I believe that only a yogi of some sort can lead life without creating scratches. The magnitude of the scratches and the magnanimity of the person involved, determine the effort required to polish it. The effort varies from smooth and subtle to mammoth and mountainous. Every scratch can be polished, every scratch leaves us with valuable lesson. Check out the quote by Mater in cars movie. I love this quote.

Every dent bears the beauty of grace and redemption

What is the scratch in your life that is stirring up some emotion inside you. Are you going to vent up your anger or drown in guilt. Neither will help.

Show your emotion with grace if you got scratched by someone.

Redeem yourself from guilt by polishing the scratch,if you are the one who scratched.

Some scratch may vanish over time. Like the scratch in the shoe. It faded away in two weeks.

Scratch vanished

If the Scratch will get healed anyway over time, Do we really need to vent our emotions and create a relay race of scratches?

A SMALL LAMP THAT MADE A BIG DIFFERENCE

What is your excuse?

"We could have scored more runs with the kind of bat the opponents had"

"Sophisticated sports equipment would have made sure that we won the match"

"Mom, I feel terrible to carry these old books. It was used at least by 10 students before it came to me. It does not even have place for me write my name. I get a foul smell from this book which makes it difficult for me to concentrate"

Definition of Life at that point in time would be :

Life = Excuses.

I was hailed as a champion cricket player. Yes. You read it

right. Champion. Though it was in the street cricket that we played. When I moved to play in the leather ball in a proper cricket ground, I failed miserably. Our team was outplayed by the opponents. Major reason—we were under-prepared. However, Human mind can create wonders. We prepared well to defend our defeat. I used to create wonderful reasons for not playing properly. Easy one is to blame the opponent teams "Sophisticated kit".

I have never failed in my studies. I have also never came out in flying colours either. I managed to stay with the crowd, in the average performance criteria. I call it the safe zone.

However, I used the best of grey matters to scuttle out reasons. One of the reasons being that the books are old. My parents could not afford to buy new books for me or for my brother. We did our studies by borrowing books from senior students known to us.

I was good at finding excuses to escape reality.

The mind produces wonderful results in the areas where it could maintain focus. To quote famous author Robin Sharma "What you focus, grows". My imagination grew in multitude to produce reason for lackluster performance.

The imagination expanded with my age to produce innovative excuses while performance keep dropping and then this happened.

I was in Grade 8. The term was about to end. The last day of the term was kept for bidding adieu from the teachers. All the teachers churns out advice after advice. We in turn give them a token gift from our side.

While we as a class remained more or less happy with all the teachers except for Mr. Kuzhandaivelu-our tamil teacher. He was great in teaching and instilling disciple but brutal in punishing. He was determined to produce tamil scholars out of each one of us. Leaving a few students, the rest of us have taken a vow to redefine the low standards in studies. So, he has ended up as an enemy for the majority in the class. We made a plan to teach him a lesson by humiliating him in front of other teachers. We bought standard gifts for all the teachers except for Mr. Kuzhandaivelu. We got a small traditional indian oil lamp (see picture) but packed it in multi-layered paper.

The day came. We gave the gift for all the teachers. While the rest of the teachers could get hold of the gift by unpacking just one layer, Mr. Kuzhandaivelu kept unpacking layer by layer. After a considerable effort he could hold on to the the small indian oil lamp. He did two things on that day that shifted my thinking. He remained calm and composed throughout the unpacking exercise. He delivered a speech that got imprinted in my mind so well that I remember the entire event clearly even after all these years.

He held the lamp in his hand, without showing any disappointment but rather displaying enthusiasm he said "I am really grateful to you guys for this wonderful parting gift. As a parting thought, I want to say that this lamp may be small in size but with the relevant material it can eradicate darkness in and around the place where it is kept. . This little lamp can not only bring light but also has the capability to lit thousand lights. I wish that all of you will become the light that shines and lights up thousand more lights"

This was an eye opener for me. Mr. Kuzhandaivelu could have used the small lamp as an excuse to scold us rather he chose to bring out the innate positiveness in the lamp.

"The idea that what you get in life does not matter but what you do with what you get in life matters" got chiseled in mind thanks to his golden words. This reiterates what Theodore Roosevelt said

"Do what you can with all you have, where you are".

That small lamp in the hands of Kuzhandaivelu sir made a big difference to the lives of most of the students in that hall. I am one among them.

The fact that I have borrowed book cannot stop me from studying hard. The path towards gaining knowledge became crystal clear. I redefined the journey in education.

The fact that I could not afford sophisticated kit does not stop me from putting my best of efforts in any sports that I played thereafter.

Even today when I stumble in a situation where my mind cries foul about what I have got in life, the voice of Mr.Kuzhandaivelu resonates in my mind and wakes me up.

It does not matter what we get in life. What makes the difference to us and people around us depends on what we do with what we get in life.

The Question is "What are we doing with what we have in our life".

Are we finding Excuses or trying to excel in life with what we have.

EMOTIONALLY CHARGED OR IN-CHARGE OF EMOTIONS

We finished our short family vacation and were getting ready to fly back. I tried mobile check and was shocked to see seat number differing from the one we chose while booking the ticket. I called the customer service. The lady on the other side laughingly said "Sir, Don't worry. Mobile check in is not considered by us. You will be issued fresh tickets at the airport counter. The seat numbers are still appearing intact. Just reach the airport on time".

That was a breather and we forgot the seat change.When we reached the airport, the counter staff gave us boarding passes with seat numbers in three different rows for three of us. When I narrated the whole story, the man behind counter apologized but only could manage three seats in a different row but seated together. The seat blocked by us were in row 16 and the one issued were in row 25. We were not happy. We insisted that row 16 is given to us. The staff went to check with someone but returned only to apologise his inability. When we persisted with our request, he referred us to the supervisor.

The conversation with the supervisor is exactly reproduced below .

Me : "Hi, I am travelling in this flight from XXX to YYY. We blocked seats while booking but the seats presently given differs completely. Is it possible to help us out".

Him : "Which airline you are travelling".

This appears to be a valid question. However, the tone in which this was thrown at me made me feel ridiculed. There is no other airline that was flying from XXX to YYY on that day other than this airline and this counter is exclusively designated for this airline. Let us take this airline as "ABC airlines"

Me : "ABC airlines of-course. I have not experienced this inconvenience in any other airlines that I have traveled in the past"

Him : I don't know about other airlines. But this cannot happen in our airlines. Please give me the details.

After checking in the system.

Him: I cannot do anything now. You have done the mobile check-in.

Me : That's exactly why I have approached you. Tell me How the seat selected can change once you check in.

Him: I cannot help. It is an IT issue. Further, you have done mobile check in already.

Me : What? Such an useless system and airline. I have never had such an experience with any other airline. I have traveled only 3 times in this airline and I had faced one or other problem which never gets a solution. There is no customer support.

Him : Please don't be rude. I am trying to help you.

Me : I am sorry if I sounded rude, but blaming IT and mobile check-in is definitely not helping me.

All this was happening when my wife intervened

My wife : "I don't how this has happened. We would be happy if we can get the same seat …."

He cut short abrasively. "I am not speaking to you"

The situation really exploded here. My wife lost her cool. I lost my cool.

Me : "I am sorry gentleman. That was rude"

After arguing for two to three minutes, he apologised for his action.

Thereafter he issued us tickets with the same seat numbers that we asked for.

This incident stuck into my head like a piece of gum in the shoe. I remembered the Manners of Starting a Conversation from the workshop that I attended few months back. The Most important aspect in striking a conversation with a new person is to introduce yourself first and get the name of the other person. I failed. I started the conversation abruptly.

I could have started the conversation differently. May be like "Hi, I am so and so. I am travelling in your airline. I have blocked seats 16 A,Band C. However, while doing mobile check-in, the seats got changed. I was told that you are the only person who can help us out in this situation. Can you please help us out".

This would have probably changed his mood.

While having conversation try to avoid negative remarks. I did manage to include few negative and mean remarks about the airline, though it is factually correct.

May be he would have been polite and asked "may I have more details" rather than asking which airline. He made me feel like a fool by asking the question "Which airline" considering the fact that no other airline is flying to the location that I was flying on that day and the counter clearly carries the name of this particular airline and all the staff displaying the logo of the airline that I was flying. He provoked me. But then I handed over control of the conversation to him by making negative remarks.

However, the conversation turned into our favour when he made the mistake of acting rude towards my wife. When he acted like a misogynist and rejected the conversation that my wife was trying to make, he lost the conversation. He gave the power in our hands.

However, I am glad that he realised his mistake and gave us the tickets we asked for though not before giving us the glimpse of rude customer service.

I may think twice before I book my next flight in that airline.

Emotional Intelligence cannot be learnt by attending seminars and classes or listening to YouTube videos. It needs to be practiced. I was emotionally charged up during the entire episode. I needed to be in Charge of the Emotion instead.

May be this will be my main resolution for 2017.

Be in control of my emotions. Be in control of the situation.

"It is never too late to be what you might have been."
– George Eliot

THE TEACHER APPEARS WHEN THE STUDENT IS READY!!!

Two things will make life beautiful, life filled with love,peace and eternal exaltation.

First thing is Gratitude. Having the Attitude of gratitude allows us to feel the innate beauty of life. Thank the Creator, thank nature, thank Mother Earth for her patience despite rampage meted out by us and thank all those wonderful people who come in our life.

Second thing is Random act of Kindness. Making it a practice to carry out that act which brings some difference to the world. I know it is difficult to practice. I don't remember when was the last time I did one. May be last week I pushed my friend to take part in a contest. Well, I was not sure whether she considered it as a random act of kindness though it appeared like I was having fun at the cost of her participation. Nevertheless at the end of the contest, she thanked me from the bottom of her heart which made me happy. The issue with the random act of kindness is that we find it difficult to instill it as a habit.

My perception changed today. This morning as I completed my walk and entered the street where I live. I saw this person who works in the laundry. He was carrying a small bowl of grains. I wished him good morning. I was curious to know what he was doing. I slowed down to watch him. He scattered those grains in the corner of the street. As he turned and walked towards his shop, I could notice flurry of pigeons dashing towards the rice. He has fed few lives in this earth. He moved quietly towards his shop to carry out his routine. Any simple act can become a Random act of Kindness when it touches lives. Feeding birds also amounts to an act of kindness. Birds cannot reciprocate their gratitude. Not at least in words!!!

"When the Student is ready, Master appears".

I was not ready for this simple lesson till yesterday. May be I am ready today and the master appeared in the form of the laundry man.

I decided carry grains while I go for walking from tomorrow. I can feed few lives each day.

FOURTH HABIT THAT I WANT TO INSTILL IN ME

The Habit of Morning Walk got instilled in me while I was young. I should be around 11 when I joined the gang of my elder brother for morning jog and Yoga. Over the years, Yoga became an on and off practice but morning walk remained as a habit.

Early days of jog was filled with fun and horror. Horror comes from the stories that were shared by seniors during jogging. One such story is about an "Headless Man" roaming around the highway (incidentally this highway is part of our jogging route). Being the youngest, I was still learning to act brave after hearing such bizarre stories. But I know acting was never my strength and my face showed the fear in my mind. Like how an hungry tiger could smell its prey, senior bully could smell victory. More the fear, more bizarre became the stories. However, I grew stronger over the years but continued the morning jog but most of the others dropped and stopped this habit. When I was alone in this pursuit, jogging turned into walking. Still today this habit stayed with me.

I learnt Yoga as well but somehow the practice remained intermittent. So I cannot call Yoga as a Habit in my schedule.

The second habit is to "Thank God" when I wake up. I don't remember when I started. This is obviously not a childhood practice. But I am doing it daily. This really makes the day brighter or at least makes me feel blessed for every experience that I go through in a day. I read somewhere that this is an habit that many successful people have in their list. I am not sure whether I can place myself with those greats, but I can sure say that starting the day with gratitude definitely makes the experience better.

The third habit which again is linked to gratitude is something that I picked up very recently. I got it through a whatsapp share. This is about thanking 10 most important people in my live for their contribution in shaping me and making me the person as I stand today. As I started doing, I find 10 is a small number but I stick to 10. The reason is simple. If I add more now as I proceed further, I may drop the entire exercise because of the time it will take. The habit will gradually vanish. So, I stick to 10. This really makes me humble and grounded. This habit reminds me everyday that I am not self-made. "I" am contribution of sacrifices of so many people around me. "I" am made of significant effort by people who cared for me. My parents taught me modesty and hardwork. My friend Raman helped me in diverting and channeling my energy towards studies. My teachers, superiors and colleagues added vital value at various points in time. My wife supported me and showed resilience to stand by me. She remains the greatest pillar of support in my life. My son brought a completely new dimension in my life. I could understand my father much better now. Showing gratitude to each of them who significantly influence(d/s) my life makes me grounded. It also provides me a sense of belonging. Above all it increases the humbleness quotient. Finally, it also gives me a push to contribute significantly to help people around me especially younger generation.

The fourth habit that I want to inculcate is "to live the present moment". Yesterday as I was completing my routine morning walk, I saw a three year old running with open arms as if she is welcoming life. Her laughter is still resonating in my ears. Her eyes were reflecting the joy and freshness of life. The curiosity in understanding things and her search for fun in every nook and corner. When she looked at me, I turned into a child. I started blinking fast. She stared at me with more joy and then she repeated. Child carries no inhibition. They are ready live the moment. But as adult we stop ourselves from living the moment. We are more concerned about what others will think of us. We are more worried about our perceived image. Forget it. The image that we want to portray and the image others perceive may differ. We feel that we portray an image of a champion but others may be seeing a bully in us. I have faced situations where people had diagonally opposite view of my behaviour compared to what I was trying to portray. So it is better to live the moment. Forget about the perception of others, just live the moment. After all, most of our life is, what we live in our mind.

What are your habits? What is the new habit you want to instill in you?

IF THERE IS SOMETHING I WANT TO CHANGE, IT IS THAT LOOK IN MY FATHER'S FACE

This happened way back in 1992. I was in the second year of my graduation. My favorite past time was to hang out with my friends.What we do..in simple terms"Nothing". In the words of my teacher "These hangouts are nothing but an exchange house of information that paves way to gaining knowledge in areas which has no significance to the persons involved nor the society"

My father defined it more simply "This is den where useless creatures wasted oxygen and space".

One such days where we were happily inhaling oxygen and exhaling so many useless ideas, my father came home without his moped. His moped stopped in the middle of a road. He had to abandon it and came by bus. He asked me to go and fetch it. I told him that I am going out with my friends but will do this in the evening. However, I conveniently forgot it. He tried to get hold of my brother but in vain as he left much earlier that day. Those were the days the mobile phone revolution has not even thought of.

I was happily enjoying with my friends and reached home late in the evening. As I approached my house I could see my father pedaling the moped towards us. He has gone himself to take the moped. It was almost 20 kms. He has pedaled it all the way. He came closer to the house. I took the moped from him and said " I would have gone in the evening". He never uttered a word, but his facial expressions spoke million words.

If there is something in the world that I want to change, given a choice, I would go back to change that chapter. I want to change the look in my father's face. I wanted to see a different me who would choose to get the TVS -Moped myself instead of hanging out with my friends.

The look in my father's face has been captured and framed in my mind. It is promptly played again and again to taunt me.

Mahatma Gandhi said "Your future is determined by the actions you take today". In other words, your action today creates the imagery for your mind to play in future.

The question is not just about the imagery we want to create about our life in our minds but also about the imagery we would like to create in the minds of people around us and closer to us.

I hope to create better experiences that can create great imagery for my mind to play back .

I am sure everyone hopes for the best.

CHOICE BETWEEN FREEDOM AND COMFORT

Tallinn view from upper old town

If the choice is between Freedom or Comfort -what will you choose?

Well, if the question was put to me when I was growing up, I would have chosen comfort (though grudgingly).

Today, I may chose Freedom with a bit of comfort attached to it.

Why am I deliberating this subject anyway.

Before I get to the why, let me take you to Tallinn, capital city of Estonia. Estonia is one of the few countries from the erstwhile soviet union to join European Union.

It is a small city with 159 km radius and just around 500 k population. 45% of the population in Tallinn speak Russian.

I visited this city as part of the stop over in the Baltic Cruise.It is a small city which preserves the history well. While the highlights of the city can be found through Google, I would like to discuss about my conversation with the tour guide Julia.

Julia was very enthusiastic and friendly lady. She possesses quite exhaustive knowledge about the city and its history. Her command over English which is an added attraction beside her pleasant appearance.

One of the fellow tourist asked her about the transition experience from soviet regime to the free market economy. She explained the amount of work the new government did in handing over the properties back to the respective owners, disputes that followed and the resolutions that emerged. It all took several years.

"Can you explain the life during soviet time?". another tourist asked.

"It also had good aspects" she continued "People got all the basic necessities without spending much. *Housing was free, everyone was assured a job* that will give them decent salary, good enough for them to buy bread not that they had other choices. People had more time to study. Art and Literature were given more time as TV programs were made available only for 2 hours. *Education and Health was taken care by the government. There was no need for people to take loans from banks and spend their lives in only repaying the mortgage.* **It definitely had its negative aspects, however one cannot dismiss it as completely bad**"

As the tour finished, I asked Julia "Given a choice, what would you choose, freedom that you enjoy today or the comfort that you had in the Soviet regime"

Julia Smiled and said "*I will choose Today. The freedom that we have today despite the struggles to earn a decent living, will outweigh all the comforts that were present in those times*"

Extending this a bit to our daily life, we choose to remain in the comfort zone in our lives. There is no other force that stops us from moving out of the comfort zone.

Move out with freedom and experience the outer limits or for that matter extend the outer limits.

We get what is necessary in the comfort zone.

But no. Don't stay there. Move out of the comfort zone.

Challenge the limits.

Break free of the self- imposed boundary.

Experience the freedom.

Unleash the creativity that can propel us to the pinnacle.

The question is What will be our choice?

LIFE IN A WALL

The first wall that inspired me was the wall in front of my house where my brother and his friends used to hang out. I was not allowed to go near the wall as my parents wanted me to focus on my studies and my elder brother wanted to keep me out in order to retain his supremacy over me .

Eventually I got the access when I finished schooling and started college education.Though my brother was bit apprehensive, his friends voted me in. I got the first opportunity to sit on the wall and gain the wisdom of youth. Well our gang consisted only boys, unlike the one that you see in the above picture. So, our wisdom or rather search of wisdom was mostly focused on girls.All the elders living in our locality used to shout at us for wasting our time by hanging out in that wall. It may be true that we would have wasted many precious hours sitting in that wall discussing about petty things. But, this wall gave us the opportunity to bond well and foster our friendship. This wall allowed us to unite despite hailing from different backgrounds, religion and even age.

I would like to call this wall a "Wall of Friendship".

The next wall that was introduced in my life was an imaginary wall. Yes. Though this happened few years before I occupied the above wall, I recognised it only after I sat on the wall of friendship.

This requires a bit of flashback. It was when I was studying on 10th grade. We are a family of fighters. We don't fight with others, but within ourselves. Mostly it was verbal except when it happens between me and my elder brother. It can turn violent. It was one of those fighting days when the verbal duel lead to hand fists. My brother being elder to me could easily subdue me. I started looking for options and got hold of the first weapon that came in contact. It was a grandfather stick. My brother started retreating and I started chasing him. He ran into the street, behind him was uncontrollable me. After almost 30 minutes of chase, I returned home feeling defeated in the chase. But that feeling ignited the anger further. I waited in the house with the stick in my hand and with the intention of making the fight even.

My mother intervened and ordered that we should stop talking to each other. It really worked wonders for both of us. There was an imaginary wall between us, brothers. We were living like strangers in the house until the day I occupied the wall. We had no option but to break this imaginary wall, else gain the wrath of all of our friends. Why? Let me give one example of our conversation.This happens between me and my brother with one or few of our friends standing as witness.

"Ask him why he did that?"-usually my brother.

"I did that because of so and so reason"-me

"Tell him that he should not do something stupid like this next time" -my brother

"Well, I will try" -me.

In the whole set of conversation, there was no involvement of the third person except that we were using them as a point of reference in our conversation.

This continued until one day when our mother asked us to

stop this nonsense and speak to each other. This imaginary wall disappeared without trace, however not before strengthening bond.

I would like to call this "Wall of Bond"

I am sure all the married couple use this imaginary wall once in a while to retreat and re-bo(u)nd stronger in their relationship.

The other Wall that I would like to delve upon is world famous "Great Wall of China". Attracting roughly 10 million visitors, this wall spans about 6300 kms but if you measure the total distance from all the sides it runs roughly about 21,600 kms. But what is available today is only 2/3rd of the original construction, the remaining 1/3rd has disappeared without trace or rather not yet traced.

This wall was built by various dynasties at different period of time but with a sole purpose. The Purpose is to fend off the enemies from attacking China.

If you look at the History of the Mankind, it appears that there were other such walls built across the world at different time period but with the similar intention. These are called Walls of borders.

Sumerian Amorite Wall, Long walls of Athens, The Great Wall of Gorgon, Hadrian's Wall, The Walls of Constantinople and Berlin Wall are some of the other walls built with the purpose of protecting the border or fending off the enemies.

I would like to call these walls "Walls of Hatred and Fear"

These Structures that were built to protect borders, stand today as a monument in history to remind us about how humans were divided by spreading fear and hatred.

Berlin Wall remains the only wall in the history that was broken down by the Human will and desire to stay united.

The wall that was built because of hatred was broken down by the power of unity, harmony and friendship.

Berlin Wall is a perfect example for triumph of love and harmony over hatred and fear. The wall which was built in 1963 to divide East and West Germany finally gave in to the power of love in 1989 and paved way for United Germany as it stands today.

The walls that we build with hatred and fear in mind, whether physical or abstract, are not going to help humanity's progress rather it will only take the world few centuries into the past.

As humans we definitely need to feel secure and protected. However, this is required only to regain our consciousness and courage. We need is an option for a temporary recluse not a permanent barrier.

Let us Break the Wall that prohibits us from moving towards future with love and friendship.

Let us choose the Wall of Friendship and Hope.

Let us choose to Unite Humanity than Divide it.

It is easier said than done. But at least keeping this as a over powering thought in every situation we face will definitely help move the world towards togetherness.

"Vasudeva Kudumbakam"-The world is one family as pronounced by the ancient Hindu Vedas is definitely a possibility within the reach of humanity.

It is decided by the choice we make.

THE GIFT

Today was the last of the Eid holidays. I was trying to catch up with the sleep that I have been deprived off. But my sleep was cut off around 7:30 in the morning when my phone rang. It was a call from an unknown number. Though bit irritated, I decided to answer the call.

I had a surprise. It was a call from Fedex.

"Hi, There is a package for you. Please give your address".

To say that I was delighted will be an understatement.

I am not sure what is in the package. It should be the order that I placed two weeks back using the Credit Card reward program.

The child in me got excited and started looking for the package. Suddenly my behavior changed like a child waiting to receive the birthday gift.

The question is what is that gift you want to give yourself today. This was the question that was posed to me in the early part of my career by one of the senior most person in that organisation. His name is P. Venkateswaran. We fondly called him PV.

PV was like a hungry lion always looking for prey, in this case prey being gaining more knowledge. Though he was heading the Materials Management, his knowledge has no boundaries. He had more than 1000 books in his collection which ranges from Finance, Economics to Science and Management. PV has made it a practice to read at least 30 minutes every day before he retires to bed. This was a practice instilled in him in his childhood. This means that he has read a minimum of 5 million pages assuming he started reading around 10 and he covers 10 pages in 30 minutes. This is the gift he has given to himself. I had the opportunity of spending few days with him. When the day was about to be called off, I have seen that glow in his face that one finds in a child that was expecting a gift. He opens the book that he has planned to read like how a child opens the gift.

Mr. PV gave me two best gifts and that too gifts that I can give myself.

First one is about reading books. He asked me to read at least 30 minutes every day. I could not read every day, but managed to incorporate the practice of reading at least 3 days in a week. But for him, I could not have read so many books that I have managed to read till date. This habit is definitely the best gift that one can give oneself.

Second being, give 100% in whatever one is doing. I still remember having an official conversation with him. I was in internal audit. I have completed the audit and was having conversation with him to finalise the audit observations. He thrashed down the points that I have raised. I was feeling bad that I failed to collect enough data to prove these points. He understood my predicament. He allowed extension of time to get the data to support my points. When I came back with the required amount of data he said "I know you were right. However, you have not given 100%. You cannot expect everyone to be like me to support you. When you take up something, give 100%, don't leave any matter open for chance. This will be the next best gift you can give yourself and the organisation you work for".

I am not sure whether I have given 100% every time, but I can definitely say that I have given my best every time which was definitely more than 100% at least in few occasions.

What is the best give you have given to yourself.

What is that activity that brings the child-like glow in your face? and How often you do that?

I get that child-like glow in my face

Every time I get an idea that can be converted into a blog

Every book that expands my knowledge base

Every idea that changes the way I work

Every opportunity to spend quality time with my family

Look for that idea or activity that brings that glow in your face. Do it often.

If that idea or activity can bring glow in the face of few people around us or connected with us, we should strive to do it more often.

Do you want to change the world, please meet Dr. Ignaz
Semmelweis before you start

Next time you get an urge to change the world, remember the
story of Dr. Ignaz Semmelweis.

For those who don't know Dr. Ignaz Semmelweis, he is the first
physician to ask fellow physicians to wash their hands before
attending another patient.

It was 1846. Physicians all over the world were left bewildered
with the fact that the mortality rate of female patients delivering
child in a hospital was more when compared to the death rate of
female patients delivering child in a home set-up with the support
of mid-wives. The difference was alarming. Five times.

It was also a period when the Physicians started probing the
causes of death to understand and progress science. Dr. Ignaz,
after completing his medicine, joined the General Hospital in
Vienna. He was interested to understand the reason behind the
death of female patients from Peurperal Fever or commonly
referred as child-bed fever.

His findings were simple though the efforts were not. The reason
-Doctors who helped in delivery of child were also involved in
autopsies. Most often, they rush from an autopsy room to delivery
room without washing their hands. These Doctors were inflicting
the patient in the delivery room with bacteria carried directly
from a dead corpse. and they won't even know of it, all the while
trying to blame the female patients or evil spirits.

If you think Dr. Ignaz Semmerlweis suggestions definitely
changed the perception. You are both right and wrong. It changed

the perception in the General Hospital in Vienna where it was adapted. But the rest of the hospitals rejected his claim.

Over time, it appears that this idea was opposed strongly by the doctor's community which left Dr. Ignaz furious and mad. Gradually, Dr. Ignaz lost his mental balance and died.

So, someone who wanted to change the world for better, died as a psychiatric patient.

However, world is not as cruel as you think. Physicians over time has realised the importance of washing hands and today the world is flooded with products which makes you wash hands every few seconds.

I came across this story in the book Superfreakonomics and did some research to confirm it.

The point here is not about Dr. Ignaz but also about us. The question is what made such a fantastic idea to be ridiculed by fellow physicians and made the person who gave the idea to die.

In my opinion, it lies in the way it was put forward. I see a major communication failure in the way Dr. Ignaz handled the message. If this message was put across in a way that avoided ridiculing the doctor's fraternity or for that matter blame them for the numerous death's that has occurred till that date, the world would have absorbed this much earlier and could have saved few more lives.

So, the effective communication is a skill that becomes an essential part in anyone's life.

Not because it would make you successful but also it could perhaps save lives.

Here I quote from Thirukkural, an ancient tamil literature written by Thiruvalluvar. It is a book with 133 Chapters with each chapter having 10 verses thus total versus amounting to 1330. This book covers diverse areas including to leadership, governance, love, family etc. Following verse on the communication encapsulates the essence of effective communication.

" A widely learned man, if cannot communicate well,

All his learning is a waste"

பல்லவை கற்றும் பயமிலரே நல்லவையுள்
நன்கு செலச்சொல்லா தார். (728)

It then becomes critical for everyone to take some formal training in improving communication skill.

I have been part of this amazing organisation called Toastmasters International and can proudly say that it has definitely helped me improve not just my communication skills but my overall personality.

Check out at www.toastmasters.org to find a club near your locality.

Next time you get an urge to change the world with a brilliant idea, remember the story of Dr. Ignaz. Learn to communicate the idea well so that the change gets implemented in your life time and also that you don't get tied up in a pole in a remote mental asylum to only lose your life for providing a brilliant idea that can eventually save the world.

NOT KNOWING

I was listening to one of the short stories by Thenkachi Ko Swamination. The story is about a sage and three men.

One day three men were walking in a thick forest. They found a sage standing in front of a tree. As a mark of respect they bowed before the sage. Sage asked them "Are you guys interested to fly. I have a magic carpet"

All of them were excited to fly. But then Sage said "There is one condition. I will ask you one question. If your answer is wrong, you will be thrown out from the magic carpet. But if your answer is honest and correct, you get the chance to complete the flight".

They accepted the condition with a hope that they can find right answers.

While they were flying over the forest, they could see one Pregnant Deer in the midst of delivering a baby. Few feet away, there was a tigress looking for food for its hungry cubs. The moment tigress saw the deer, the inevitable happened.

The sage now looking at these men asked "Tell me whether tiger killing deer is right or wrong"

One of them who thought he was the wisest among the three

spoke first "Tiger is right, because it is the nature of the tiger to kill. Moreover, it has to kill to feed its cubs".

Next moment, he was thrown out of the carpet. The second person immediately said "Tiger is wrong. How can someone be cruel to deer which has just delivered a baby".

Next moment, he was thrown out of the carpet. The sage turned towards the only person left out. The third person said "I don't know".

Sage and that person safely completed their trip.

The moral of the story is that people who accept that they don't know or have answers for all the questions complete their journey succesfully.

In my case, may be this helped me to successfully start my journey in corporate career.I got the first job offer in a Major Conglomerate in India with an answer "I don't know".It was the final round of interview with Director Finance. This person was a six foot well built highly knowledgeable person. When he looks at you, his eyes pierces through you and makes you feel naked. After few questions on various subjects, he threw that question which unsettled me completely.

"What is your favorite subject"

"Taxation "(Most of the Indian Chartered Accountants at that time had tax as their favorite subject).

"Well, As you are aware that the new government has just taken over. They are about to announce the Budget for the year. What recommendations would you like to provide to the Finance Minister to include in the amendments"

Startled, I could see how I managed to dig the grave for myself. I took few minutes to compose myself, swallowed the pride that I had about my knowledge in taxation and then said.

"I don't know".

I paused only to continue "I cannot make any recommendations just like that to Finance Minister. In my opinion, tax amendments needs to studied carefully considering the implications across the industries and society before including in the proposal. I need time"

I was not sure whether this answer got me the job, till few years later when I had the opportunity to attend the meetings with the Managers and Directors. They had no fear in accepting that they don't know about something but took time to read about the subject/case only to get back with complete history and action plan.

Famous Tamil Poet "Avvaiyyar" said -"What we learnt is equal to handful of sand, but what is still to be learnt is about the size of the world"

That's truly humbling. The realisation that we don't possess complete knowledge leads us to an humbling experience.

STORY OF YOU, ME AND US

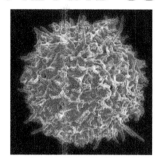

The amazing facts about how a single cell transforms into a full grown human body in 9 months really fascinated me.

I was sitting inside a dimly lit, air-conditioned five star conference room, listening to lecture on human wellness. The thrilling concept that I wrote in the opening line was well defined and I was enthralled when I heard that the entire blue print of how this human body has to take shape is contained in that one cell. It is a four letter story called GENE. Any mistake in this four letter or any letter wrongly placed in order may potentially change the entire life story of that single cell.

Wait…I am not a science student. So, I am not going to delve into more scientific terms, though they are interesting and captivating. I am interested in the idea of the story.The beautiful story that we are. The brilliant story that we turn out to be in those 9 months. But, those were only the first few chapters of the story. The rest remains as a blank page to be filled in by us. The story, should it remain fascinating, captivating, enthralling and enduring is completely left with the individual.

God Almighty or Nature has done their job when the initial part of your story was written without an error.

To take the story forward is left to us.

So, the question is What is the story so far?

What is the Story that we want it to be from now on?

Will it be a sad and boring one…or

Will   it
be   riveting,spellbinding,entrancing,mesmerizing,scintillating,
radiant, majestic,astounding one.

It is left to us to decide.

Printed in Great Britain
by Amazon

39167945R00030